I Am, Because...

CAROLYN WATSON

Copyright © August 2023 by I Am, Because

Carolyn Norman-Watson

All rights reserved.
No part of this publication may be reproduced, distributed, or transmitted in any form by any means, including photocopying, recording, or other electronic methods without the prior written permission of the publisher, except in the case of brief quotations embodied in reviews and certain other noncommercial uses permitted by copyright law.

For permission requests, write to the publisher at the following address:

Posley GLOBAL LLC
PO Box 20
Glenwood, IL 60425
www.PosleyGlobal.com

ISBN: 978-1-7348994-8-1

Printed in the United States of America

Publisher:
Posley GLOBAL LLC

*Thank you for choosing this poetry book.
We appreciate your support and
hope you enjoy the poems within its pages.*

ACKNOWLEDGEMENT

In the enchanting world of poetry, there are rare moments when a collection transcends the boundaries of time and space, leaving an indelible mark on the hearts and minds of its readers. "I Am, Because" by Carolyn Norman-Watson is one such masterpiece that invites us to embark on a soul-stirring journey through the depths of human emotions and the vast landscapes of the human experience.

Within the pages of this remarkable collection, Carolyn Norman-Watson weaves together a tapestry of words that illuminates the complexities of identity, love, and resilience. Her poetic prowess effortlessly captures the essence of what it means to exist in a world filled with both joy and sorrow, hope and despair.

Born and raised in the southern states of Alabama, Florida, and Georgia, Carolyn's unique perspective on life is deeply rooted in her diverse background. From her early days in the bustling city of Atlanta to her later years in the vibrant cultural hub of California, Carolyn's journey has shaped her poetic voice, infusing her verses with a raw authenticity that resonates with readers of all walks of life.

Through her evocative imagery and lyrical musings, Carolyn invites us to reflect on our own experiences, to embrace the power of self-discovery, and to find solace in the beauty that surrounds us. Her words serve as a gentle reminder that even in the midst of life's trials, our true essence remains untarnished, our spirit unyielding.

"I Am, Because" is not merely a collection of poems; it is a celebration of the human spirit, a testament to the power of words to heal, inspire, and connect us all. Carolyn Norman-Watson's legacy as a brilliant poet and profound observer of life shines brightly within these pages, inviting us to pause, to reflect, and to discover the profound truths that lie within our own hearts.

So, dear reader, immerse yourself in the captivating world of "I Am, Because," and allow Carolyn Norman-Watson's poetic genius to transport you to a realm where words dance and emotions intertwine. Let her masterful storytelling and profound insights awaken the dormant poet within you, and may this collection serve as a guiding light on your own journey of self-discovery and self-expression.

Shaunwell Posley,

Author and Editor

CONTENTS

Acknowledgement 5
   Seasons of Friendship 8
   My Point of View Love---------What Is It?........................ 10
   The Sentinel Rose (In Memory of Chris Hopkins Sept 1997).... 12
   The Sufficient Day 14
   Forget Me Not 16
   Crepe Myrtle and Molasses 18
   Things Past and Things to Come 20
   Anticipation 22
   Hindsight 24
   Shadows of the Past 26
   Prisms of Delusion 28
   Reasons 30
   I am, Because 32
   Royalty 34
   I am Happy and Free 36
About the Author 38

Seasons of Friendship

To be touched by a summer breeze and kissed by a snowflake flake of winter. To be awakened by a springtime of hope and fall into life again, mending a broken heart.

To be grateful to a friend who helped me to understand and appreciate the different seasons that are a part of colorful tapestry this is memory.

The delicate strokes of the brush that painted the wonderful memories on my heart will always be cherished, and the painting will forever hang on a special wall in my mind.

After all this time, an unexpected encounter that brought closure and fruition to incredible and improbable fantasies.

Ahhh, the single red rose...

P.S. I tip my hat to you, my friend.

My Point of View Love---------- What Is It?

Love is awakening to a new day
Knowing that the smile on our face
Will shower the world with sunshine.

Seeing you, touching you, wanting
With all my heart to belong to you
To look at you someday and say with
All truth.....YOU'RE MINE.
The masculine, yet gentle sway of your body
As you walk toward me to say Good Morning
As we have been apart the sleeping hours
Of the night.

To know that soon you will ask me if
We can spend a quiet evening at home
To relax, enjoy, and learn little things
About each other that, perhaps, will
Enhance and strengthen our relationship.

Dreaming the impossible dream...
To capture the beautiful illusive
Butterfly of love with an invisible net
Of affection, but with a very real heart
That pounds out your name with every beat.

Reaching out with desperation
To grasp just a small portion of the
Ecstasy of knowing that our lives
Slightly touched.

Granted: love is a condition of the mind
But so conditioned by the strong, unrelenting
Persuasion of the heart.

The prayer I say when I ask God to guide
The arrow from Cupid's bow to gently pierce
Your heart so that you will want to touch
My life with true affection.

I stand without beauty, without anything to
Offer except my pleading heart and the
Emptiness that my arms surround...
Wanting, and patiently waiting as I ask
Myself what love is. It's really quite simple...

LOVE IS WHAT I SEE WHEN I LOOK AT YOU.

The Sentinel Rose
(In Memory of Chris Hopkins Sept 1997)

A petal has fallen from a rose
That was planted in the garden of life.

I knew the warmth and love of my family,
But from the world, I learned strife.

You watch the clouds of buttermilk sky
Drift away to reveal azure blue.

You watch the starry night sky,
As humans want to do.

There is a star that twinkles to say:
I only stayed a short time on Earth,
Now, I can help watch over you.

Why now, Dear Lord, you wonder,
put your faith to this test?
The answer is quite simple you see
GOD CALLED ME HOME TO REST!

Listen. A voice whispers in quiet repose:
"A petal has fallen from a rose..."

The Sufficient Day

Fluffy white clouds in an azure blue sky
Vapor trails of jets that go zooming by

Birds fluttering from tree to tall tree
Providing food and protection for a young family

Squirrels chasing acorns to take to their nest
Preparing for winter and well deserved rest

Spring has sprung and the animals are awake
To an enlivened Earth and a beautiful new day

Treetops swaying in a fierce sumner breeze
Snapping like coach whips in Victorian days of ease

Whips saying to horses: "HURRY! On your way!'
To bring a lovely ending to a picture perfect day

To end this day with a prayer of thanksgiving
For life and serenity here among the living

I am thankful for blessings bestowed upon me
And in my heart You can plainly see

Your grace is sufficient for me. Amen.

Forget Me Not

I thought all was lost til you came along
And put love in my heart and it burst into song

A song of joy, of laughter and cheer
And hopes you'd love me forever my dear.

What can I say? What can I do?
Life would be empty without you.

I'm thankful to God happiness has come my way
With you beside me, my happiness will stay.

Missing you, wanting you, my ever present desire.
Please hurry to me and light my dying fire.

I've been yours since the day we first met.
I will love only you WHATEVER comes---DON'T FORGET!

Crepe Myrtle and Molasses

The Crepe Myrtle bush guarding the front
The Molasses standing sentry in the back
Crepe Myrtle and molasses-a soothing balm
For these frequent nostalgia attacks.

When the day was done and supper finished
When everyone was at ease
We'd all gather on Grandpa's back porch
To watch the moon rise above the trees.

A beautiful sight, the "ol' man in the moon"
Who will watch over us during the night.
We'd ask God to keep us in His care
As we planned a tomorrow that'd be "outta sight".

We'd rise and shine like that "lucky ol' sun"
To enjoy another great day.
Molasses, biscuits and fried fatback
Would supply our energy along the way.

Romping and playing with our old dog, Collie,
Chasing uncles up chinaberry trees,
Disturbing hornets' nests, meddling barnyard animals,
Skillfully dodging angry bumble bees.

Well, vacation is over 'cause summer has ended.'
We kids stand around with tears in our eyes,
Wondering, though fruitlessly,
"Why can't vacation time be extended?"

Childhood memories come and go,
Mine are not torn or twisted.
Just a few nostalgic words to show
A lovely childhood revisited!

Thinking of Crepe Myrtle and Molasses
How wonderfully we've been blessed
The general consensus of the group:
"We'll see you all at Christmas!!"

Things Past and Things to Come

The night was young when you
Held me in your arms

The night was yours when
You thrilled me with your charm

OH, how I long to be with you again
Just your touch, to want it-Is it a sin?

Just for the enchantment of
Your tender kiss

To feel the ecstasy, to see, its heavenly bliss.

All through the years you whispered to me
Bitter sweet things and how we should be.

Then, I didn't believe, took you as a flirt.

Now that I know the truth darling, it hurts.

The things that you told me and how you could wait—

Now that I realize it, let's hope it's not too late.

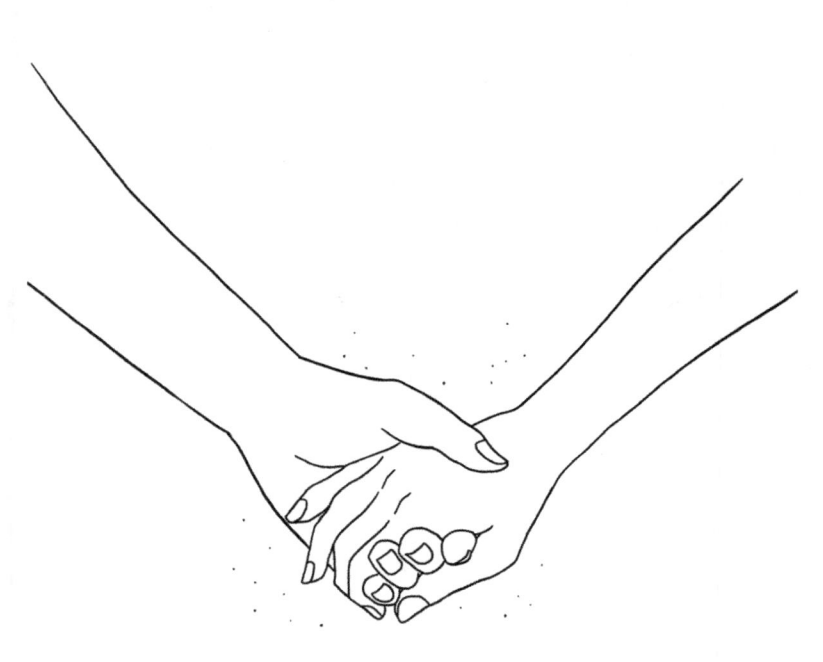

Anticipation

For such a long time I was asleep emotionally.
To feel youthful and vibrant again never occurred to me.
Then you came along and put a spark into my existence.

A thought. A memory. A daydream.

I think of how you touched me, remembering your kiss.
I think of how you held me. I remember how we walked arm in arm, going no place in particular, daydreaming of forever.

Because of you, I feel like a rosebud waiting to bloom, waiting to feel the dew drops on the petals of my face.
Because of you, I want to experience the garden of life.

Because of you, here I am...waiting.

Hindsight

I see the winds of change and the sands of time forming the silvery seashore.

I see the blue waters of wonder washing over the skeletons of lonely heartaches.

On the horizon of reality, I see love songs and happiness taken away by the empty hopes of the future.
I see myself standing on the beach-
Holding a bottle of broken dreams.

Shadows of the Past

A WHISPER
A TOUCH
A CARESS
A KISS
MEMORIES OF YOU
I CANNOT DISMISS

YOU WILL FOREVER REMAIN
SPECIAL TO ME
A PLACE IN MY HEART
YOU WILL ALWAYS KEEP.
FOR YOU
FROM ME

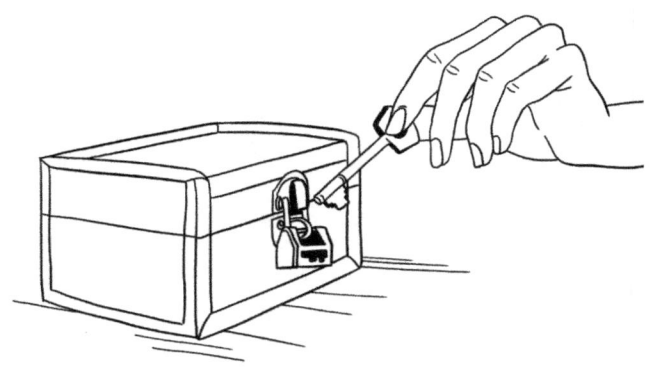

Prisms of Delusion

A chance meeting, a close encounter.
A touch, a smile, a tentative embrace.
A brush of the lips, a kiss of promise.

A whisper of possibilities.
A thought, a memory, a daydream.

A sound of music that enfolds each multi-hued
Prism that falls from the gossamer wings of the
Ever illusive butterfly of love.

A pause…to reflect.

Reasons

When you need instructions on leading a life that's good
Refer to the Good Book for it will show you how.
The words were true way back when, and are true now.
There is wisdom on how to cope with every situation,
Just read, absorb the spiritual knowledge from Genesis to Revelations..
Placed in a manger, the day he was born, a place here the animals were fed.
No room for the weary travelers to rest, therefore, no room for a baby's bed.
God sent His only son to help us find salvation. He opened his heart, held out His hands
As he walked and talked about God's love to every nation.
Thirty-three years Christ was on this earth enduring hatred, rejection, and treason.
So when we celebrate Christmas and Easter, if for no other reason, let us remember
That God's son, Jesus Christ, is the reason for both seasons.

My God is an awesome God! His wonders we do behold!
From the dawn of time, to the present day, as in the days of old-
We find that the Holy Bible, the Good Book, is the greatest story ever told!

I am, Because...

I AM,
BECAUSE MY HEART BEATS.
I AM,
BECAUSE I BREATHE
I AM,
BECAUSE I SEE.
I AM,
BECAUSE I LEARN.
I AM,
BECAUSE I APPRECIATE.
I AM,
BECAUSE I LOVE.
THEREFORE I AM, BECAUSE GOD IS.

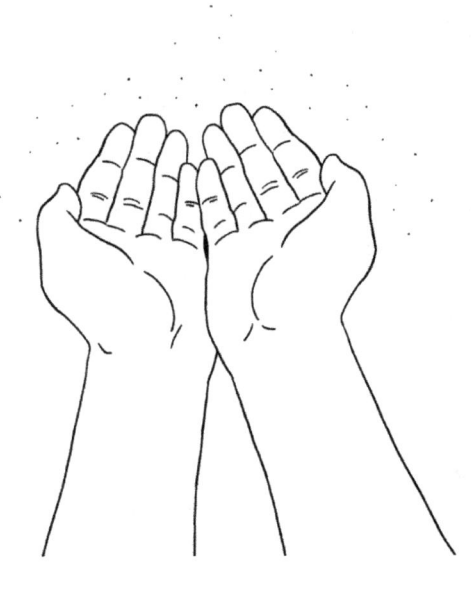

Royalty

Purple robes and golden gowns,
Precious jewels to adorn a crown.
These earthly things can never be
What the love of God means to me.

Lord of lords and king of kings,
To be His child is everything.
I shall not want, need or go astray,
For His help is but a prayer away.

So open up your hearts and let Him in,
For that is when life truly begins!

When I wake to a shiny new day
I give thanks for another delay.
Father, Son, and Holy Ghost
Of this day I will make the most.

No purple robes or golden gowns,
No jewels on an ornate crown.
Our Father is king, and forever will be
We are all members of THE royal family.

I am Happy and Free

I am Happy and Free
I am traveling the path God laid for me.

I took His hand
When I heard Him call
I turned my back on the world and all.

I had to stop, think, work and pray
And now I find sweet peace at the close of each day.

If when I am gone leaves a void
Then fill it with remembered joys.

A friendship shared, a laugh or kiss
Those things I too shall miss.

Be not burdened with long time sorrow
Remember the sun will shine tomorrow.

My Life has been full
And I have savored much
Good friends, good times
And love one's touch.

But now I can see the setting of the sun
Just listening to hear my God say, "Well Done".

Perhaps my time may have seemed all too brief
Please don't lengthen it with undue grief.

Lift up your heart
And peace be to thee
God will call me soon
I am Happy and Free.

'Nellie Norman'

ABOUT THE AUTHOR

Carolyn Norman-Watson, the late author of "I Am, Because," left behind a remarkable posthumous poetry collection that reflects her wealth of life experiences and diverse background. Growing up in the southern states of Alabama, Florida, and Georgia, Carolyn's formative years shaped her perspective on life and ignited her passion for the arts.

After graduating from Lomax-Hannon High School in 1964, Carolyn moved to California to pursue a career in acting. She attended East Los Angeles College and immersed herself in theatrical arts, honing her skills on stage. While pursuing her passion, Carolyn also worked in the corporate sector, dedicating 26 years to a career in the Standard Oil Corporate office as an Analyst.

Throughout her journey, Carolyn continued to nurture her love for writing and poetry. She became a published author, captivating readers with her evocative words and profound insights into the human experience. Even after her passing, Carolyn's talent and dedication to her craft live on through "I Am, Because," a collection that showcases her unique voice and poetic prowess.

"I Am, Because" is a poignant posthumous collection of Carolyn Norman-Watson's poetry, which encapsulates her diverse experiences and deep understanding of the human condition. Through her heartfelt verses, Carolyn invites readers to embark on a poetic journey that explores themes of identity, love, resilience, and the beauty found in the everyday moments of life.

Although Carolyn is no longer with us, her legacy as a prominent voice in the literary world remains. Her posthumous collection, "I Am, Because," serves as a testament to her enduring impact and the transformative power of her words.

Nellie Chapman-Norman, a former teacher and mother of three, is the extraordinary poet behind the inspiring poem "Happy and Free." Graduating college during a tumultuous period in American history, Nellie's journey is a testament to her strength and determination.

Born in 1920, Nellie experienced firsthand the hardships brought on by the Spanish Flu pandemic and the heartbreaking Tulsa, Oklahoma massacre that ravaged the African American community. Despite the challenges she faced, Nellie pursued her education and became a teacher, using her knowledge and passion to empower young minds.

Nellie's poem, "Happy and Free," not only reflects her personal experiences but also encapsulates the struggles and triumphs of a generation. Her words are imbued with wisdom and hope, reminding us that amidst adversity, happiness and freedom are choices we can make.

As a mother of three, Nellie's love and dedication to her family shine through in her poetry. Her words resonate deeply, inspiring readers to cherish the simple joys in life and to embrace the freedom that comes from within. Nellie's unwavering spirit serves as a beacon of light, guiding us through the darkest of times.

Today, at the remarkable age of 103, Nellie Chapman-Norman continues to inspire through her poetry. Her journey, from a college graduate during a tumultuous era to a cherished mother and teacher, is a testament to the power of resilience and determination. "Happy and Free" is a profound addition to this collection, showcasing the extraordinary talent and spirit of Nellie Chapman-Norman.

www.ingramcontent.com/pod-product-compliance
Lightning Source LLC
Chambersburg PA
CBHW072138070526
44585CB00016B/1732